OKAPI

First published in 2024 by Blue Diode Press
30 Lochend Road
Leith
Edinburgh EH6 8BS
www.bluediode.co.uk

ISBN: 978-1-915108-23-4

Typesetting: Rob A. Mackenzie & Amy Curtis
text in Pilgrim LT Roman

Cover photograph: Fiona Moore
Cover design and typography: Rob A. Mackenzie & Amy Curtis

Diode logo design: Sam and Ian Alexander.

Printed and bound by Imprint Digital, Exeter, UK.
https://digital.imprint.co.uk

OKAPI

Fiona Moore

BLUE DIODE PRESS
EDINBURGH

Scholars, I plead with you,
Where are your dictionaries of the wind, the grasses?
– *Norman MacCaig*

Okapi

was my best word my favourite creature
her graceful stripey oddness went with her name
I said it and said it
playing with my plastic zoo putting her
alongside leopard   zebra   lion   giraffe
whose bright patterns on the carpet's worn savannah
made the world that began to age at my birth

bright too was my grandparents' lawn
thick with miniature flowers from which sprang
between each mowing
daisies I picked for chains
stroking their petals tipped with the cochineal
granny mixed into her apple snow

*

into the view   into the view
when our first car
topped a hill

one landscape replaced by another
scenes pulled in and out
of a cardboard theatre

*

reading wordsworth's prelude at school
resisting it   looking for my mother's initials

among layers of blackened letters
carved in the wooden table we sat round
my ear my inner being were astonished
embarrassed   to recognise my younger self
mackerel fishing by moonlight under the sgurr's bulk
our wake patterning the glitter path
long radius of the night

by day and in dreams that island
lay in sea that could take all colours of the rainbow
beyond it unrolled a frieze of mountains
steep as fairy castles
on the far side   were there
more islands   pale shadows   floating
out of a blue-gold haze

summer after summer
children met and roamed and swam
mined seams of shells for cowries
and miniature scallops bright pink or orange
dappled like sunlight on sand underwater
we jumped foamy chasms by the pier
watching for the mainland ferry
when supplies were tossed and people leapt
over a gap of heaving sea   that might widen
between big boat and small

our lamps had shades of flowered glass
round the gas mantles' twin suns
and see-saw pull-chains with metal discs
letter-punched ON and OFF
    careful with the match
as with the gentle craneflies
that fizzed against cupped hands

divers nested on a hill loch's islet
long-necked and low in the rippling water
their throats a red cascade

short-sighted   indifferent to most birds
I learnt each flower from eyebright to gentian
cinquefoil to saxifrage to the white half-globes
of grass of parnassus veined with green
and where to hear seal-song
echo up a green gap in the cliffs
with a gale that knocked me over
or how to find among shifting waves
a steady triangle   fin of a basking shark

brindled spiders webbed my reading ledge
where I was queen of sea and mountains
shipping and weather and island life passing

*

queen I might be called
inside the paper pyramids
of school fortune tellers

or skinny old witch or
mermaid with seaweed hair
but this island fortune

not that I knew   the half of it
was graspable   as heather
on a steep sheep track

or the brown-tasselled rushes
we'd peel trying not to
break their white tube of pith

*

once the forecast was wrong   did we nearly drown
me clinging to the edge of the open hold
balanced on a fish-box so I could look
over the top to track each impossible
climb up up up and
up a wave that blocked the sky   each
lurch into a trough   walled by grey water
and check the wheelhouse window
the captain's face swaying like a pendulum
his smile of concentration

all year the island would be with me
the foghorn's echo note when the mainland
had gone adrift   ceilidhs strip-lit
in the prefab hall or firelit in houses
buttercup daisy blossom and beauty
whose red-gold flanks were sweet with milk and cowpat
mcewans beer cans dropped at the roadside
the gaelic lilt   song of the postmistress
intoning numbers as she worked the switchboard

a scramble up the sgurr's steep side
far above ruins of the cleared village
learning that scree makes each footstep circular
that beyond drumming-in-the-ears
silence fills the air with a waiting sound
by the overhung ledge with a collapsed stone wall
to stop who or what falling off

into the sea-filled view
how long ago   and was it
a cosy place to sleep or a place of fear

our mother's divebombing terror of a kite
wayward as an oracle
made from flowery offcuts and bamboo
the yearly dramas of our calor gas running out
and gales cancelling the ferry
which I willed to happen each time we had to leave

heather pollen kicked up into smoke
among bumblebees on the moor's purple ocean
each year I'd take a sprig home
so we'd have to return
and sniff its honey until the florets scattered
dried beads among fluff in my pocket seams

once they hauled a sheep into our rowing boat
its waterlogged head at my feet   mouth ajar
white foam oozing from its nostrils

we dissected an ox heart that reeked of blood
at school and drew map after map of australia
diagrams of the atomic structure of elements
and the reproductive organs of flowers
none of it was interesting
it felt as if something in me had failed
the flowers   but how I cursed the universe
for its atoms   none of it fitted together

*** *** ***

sun and shadow pass over the hillside and away
over and away
turning the pages of a book

each day turns as lightly   so fast
soft light on grass   a spring so pale
it can't unlock from winter

black-legged lambs with white kneecaps
are learning quickly to jump
that they can only go so high
                        maybe a little higher

the less each day contains   the faster
skeleton of a leaf sped along
by the very thought of wanting it

heavier   slower   fuller
rustle of its past on a tree
here where so few trees take root

between the gales   the hunger
of sheep and deer
the thin soil and the sea

*

can we do the sublime again now we're losing it
tripping up or skidding can happen
any time   here in limbo
crossing overgrown lazy-bed ridges and
sloshing through waterlogged ditches
years of labour turned to bog

it helps to approach the terrain slant
climbing lumpy hills that run in waves
haphazardly as if the island had formed
from its own wild seas
spumy with winter-blackened heather

nothing sublime about the walking
unless our upright stance can even now
stand for the grandeur of humanity's achievements
which tend to exclude glacier-sized
chunks of history   now getting unfrozen
while we're busy committing our next crimes

*

long after the first island
in the hard years before its people bought it out
I went back
with a boyfriend who didn't like bad weather
the pull-chains on the gas lamps were broken
the wild rose that used to frame the door
deep pink and bee-beloved
smelling of golden-stamened heaven
had gone   and by the gate the windswept fuchsia
was shedding thin dark leaves

as for the woods up from the pier
close-pressed company along the winding track
smelling of wild garlic   pine needles   damp soil
the woods gaped a landscape of splinters
their raspberry bushes we'd picked so often
were destroyed   the farm in disrepair
dead those elders whom the grown-ups had
drunk whisky with or tea
our playmates long left

long after the first island and far away
daily reader of the financial times   stumbling
on dynamited rock   roads to nowhere
old forest paths smashed for EU funding scams
or taken aback by the unswimmable
opaque turquoise of a bauxite tailings lake
I began to question GDP

why did it take half a lifetime
more than half to think myself into
the colourful legginess of oystercatchers
in a feather-lifting breeze
and flinch at each tree cut down
to stop scorning my mother's middle-aged
desire to identify trees in winter
and save milk-bottle tops for the guide dogs

more than half for the shock of walking
an east anglian estuary dyke
snake-line of black cuneiform on the map
topped with green footpath dashes
only to find the path vanish in water

*

now I'm crossing fields to the beach   unable
not to step on flowers that came back
after an early hay harvest and then
barefoot across the cool sand   avoiding
each mound formed round a clump
of marram grass or silvery sea thistle
each one a chance to remake the dunes
breached not long ago by human feet
for gales and high tides to flatten

*

in profile
swimming in line
on sapphire sea

gold feathers
sweeping
back from each eye

liveried in chestnut
and dark grey
   how not to see

an ancient mural of
precious assets
a keeping account

five slavonian grebes
the next day three
four   two   gone

*

beyond field-boundaries the machair
runs riot   buttercups   hawkweed   red and white clover
preposterously steepled bright purple orchids
green pincushion buds of scabious
yolk-yellow birdsfoot trefoil
vetches twining   yarrow   bees   a few butterflies
ragged robin and campion the same sharp pink

skylarks and meadow pipits sing
where gentian and candy-striped bog pimpernel
grow on the headland grazed short by black cattle
epic on the skyline   under wheeling crows

at the deserted caravan site
through dune-grass white with daisies
two plain green lines mark a track
which a few weeks back was two lines of daisies
through plain green grass

at a bay on the walk to the ancient chapel
near the dune-sunk SUV crammed with bags of sheepfeed
one wheel hung over nothing
arctic terns swoop   scold and
divebomb   knife-throwing red beaks

*

a grab-bag of gull cries
heart-haunting calls
of redshank   lapwing   oystercatcher

that mimic longing for this to last
forever   sea   sky
undulation of hills and water

*

grass-heads flip white to mauve in the light
wind that grows to snatch gatepost conversations

hard enough in beginner's gaelic   madainn mhath
ciamar a tha sibh   with indulgent neighbours
elders   deep holders of history and song
whose language weaves a net to cast
across landscape and crofting seasons
   without having to shout   tha i gaothach an-diugh
tha gu dearbh   last year they were hearing a corncrake
crex crex at night in the marsh   they miss it
keeping them awake

long fine days   and the midges barely out
meeting and hill-walking are not permitted but
a beach carpark not visible from the road
empty for months   is full one fine saturday

two crofters catch up over a glass of red
leaning on a sheep fank gate   their long shadows
striping my track home from a day in the hills

the islands are closed   very few cases
nobody has died   yet   elsewhere

*

when there's a swell too rough to swim
I walk along the atlantic shore
ears full of thunder   shaped to a pounding beat
face misted in spray   feet gaming the ripples   and try
to grasp the fires elsewhere
watching huge waves rise   through binoculars

each time there comes that dread   a physical pressure
starting at heart and stomach   moving
down to the gut and limbs

up to a tightening of the forehead
the mouth-muscles   don't make a face the wind
will change

*

each breaker's blue vitrine
appears empty
until the next one

contains a seal
sunlit
pale grey-green

head down tail up flippers wide

holding
still
suspended

before the crash   the fall
when it vanishes
in foam

a head bobs up   the seal surfs again

could this be the same seal
whose beak-punctured corpse
smells briny

is it that the dead smell of sea
or the sea
of its dead

*

my partner used to say if he was dying
his worst regret would be not knowing
what would happen in the world   and then
he was dying   young

our childhood present was already
an idyllic past   a pastoral
that lost its imagined innocence in fields
of ruminating cows and bare
uplands of hungry sheep   what will be
round the next bend over the next hilltop
beyond a life that feels like it's forerunning
our collapse   both spans once without end

if we get through   how   how depleted
will the world be on the other side
what kind of language
which parts of ours will decay into thinning soil

will my okapi still have a forest
will the forests still have okapi
solitary   treading hidden paths
or will her image survive on banknotes
rotting in an unretrieved hoard

will our successors view us as the latest
in a tattered line of doomsday cults
or the prisoners who knew life only from shadows
cast on a cave wall by flames
or as we see ourselves
in the islanders who felled the last tree
or the dog that one day found a gap in the fence

faced its snarling enemy and
ran on along its own side barking as usual
pretending nothing had changed

*

the view realigns
on the walk
down to the sea

igneous hills
impossibly long cooled
from a fiery mangling

scar in the headland
where the crofter
digs out sand for sale

metamorphic rock
striped with pink brown and cream
gneiss

yellow plastic bottle half-choked in beige sand
a thick black X
on its sea-worn label

*

today the shallows are incarnadine
with seaweed   sewage-sharp up the nose
and like borscht to wade through
the sea a fierce blue further out
has lost its innocence

*

the surf beach faces west
out to the ocean
the swimming beach north to hills
between them juts a headland slashed by deep geos
where pent-up waves slop and gurgle underfoot
even in today's calm
when razorbills float on the bay's pale green water
sunlight catching their white bellies and the red of
a diver's long throat moulting to ash-grey

one great northern's still resplendent in a collage
of bridget riley op art   her black and white phase
all year they patrol the bay's outer reaches
hard not to think of them as
life-guards for human swims
looping over to dive   upping and looping
diving   and upping

august september and the sea so clear
is almost not cold
but within it lurks a nightmare
from the time when all dreams were wordless
when terrors had no name
a gelatinous dome with tawny seaweed arms
and yards-long tentacles   envenomed
the lion's mane

on the walk back   salt-haired and euphoric
how harebells glow in the machair
and oxeye daisies and meadowsweet
and dark round seedheads of knapweed

how the new moon startles over the hill's edge
the evening star a hang-glider
swung above its canopy

*

if there had been a steep drop
if the road hadn't been empty
if there had been passengers

if the seat belt hadn't held
if there hadn't been a ditch shaped to fit the roof
if dark had already fallen

if a window hadn't shattered
if no-one had come by
if the road had run next to water

***   ***   ***

late autumn on the east side and each day up
the rock-face above the new house   squelching uphill
past the lochan squeezed between two cliffs
    up   to the old township boundary fence
topped with swags of rusty barbed wire

lifting open the decayed picket gate
that stands askew in an amber pool
crossable on stones fallen off a wall
    up   to summit after summit of bare rock

from here the world curves away
a stony coastline deeply indented
by sea lochs scattered with islets

grey cliffs limit the sea's horizon
with jagged scissor-cuts across the sky
and beyond them in clear weather
a chain of triangles fades northward
faint as tracing paper
to the south-west   a sea gap   a lopsided hill

all spanned by the light that sky casts to sea
and sea to sky   pewter   silver   steel   gold
a hoard against winter

trace and retrace   dropping down
below the view towards a hill-bound
section of sea loch   guided by stone
accumulations from wall or sheep fank
or blackhouse   reminders
of the shock and long suffering of islanders
evicted from the fertile west side
to this terrain of rock and bog

later to star as jupiter
when 2001 was science fiction
its topography morphed into a maze of red
half-molten in the gassy heat

in real-world rain
it has a silvery once-futuristic gleam
perforated by lochans   each its own shape
each a landmark only from above
the opposite of an island

*

loch of the small tree
fank loch
loch of the red-throated diver who may still nest there

inlet or heel loch
loch of the narrows
road loch

loch of sorrow or the axle tree or possibly the haystack
long-backed loch
grey fank loch

loch of the lame cow
shieling loch
loch of the black wether

loch of young iain's shieling
gull loch where they used to congregate
loch of the big hill

russet fank loch
loch of the tree
dreadful or ugly loch   a dark wedge in the bedrock

loch of the stone slabs
black loch
laundry loch

*

two weatherbeaten window-frames
in the roofless cottage closest to home

and a single pane of glass
loose and rattling

a high-crowned metal rain hat
on a fence corner-post that marks one way
downhill avoiding crags and the wettest bog

rain can reveal the wood's internal structure
rotting away the softer parts first
a snowflake spans the hollow in one gatepost
and another fragrant with rot inside
lined with moss and curly pale green lichen
recreates a childhood dream of flying
overland into a crater   softly down
past our grandparents' leafy suburbia
houses and trees clinging to the vertical sides
into feathery darkness

*

my partner is visiting in dreams again
maybe an isolation syndrome
along with the realisation that if there's enough
going on in your head
you can make a drama of any household thing
pace around for the oven to reach bread temperature
while watching the weather act on the colours
of sea loch and hills
each heating-up oven has its own smell

or explore obsessions such as wanting
to do or eat things in uneven numbers   but
if you add two unevens you get an even
of course you can add

even + uneven = uneven
either way you can't keep out the evens

*

news comes to us
as particles
blown onshore

rain
reinvents itself
against the glass

*

tasks circle like planes in a holding pattern
planes here now are a rarity
high silver darts from elsewhere

diving into elsewhere each day is easy to #belarus
not august's wide boulevards where thousands swarmed but
apartment block yards   snowy and half-lit
where people with white-and-red scarves and umbrellas
unfold a white-red-white flag
march and chant   for 20 seconds

a thicket of hashtags   doomscroller gif
screenlit face against rembrandt-dark background
jerking chin and eyes up   grimace and
a finger-flick to swat villains   oh for more
graffiti from the filth of ancient rome
that age of satirists and real scrolls

syria myanmar covid19 yemen
#reclaimthesestreets #blacklivesmatter
is anywhere elsewhere any more
outside this piebald landscape

the sea loch's bright slash darkens the hill behind it

how many birds is the single black guillemot
wintering on its waters

*

what a time this is
amid silence
to document small domestic hatreds

burnt toast   its smell and taste
stinking of the road
the greasiness of scrapings in the sink

how the two edges of butter-paper
once opened   won't overlap
though there is now less butter inside

a time to savour   very slowly
extra dark chocolate
molten between palate and tongue

or gaze at a photo someone took
of elsewhere   sent
in the spirit of never again perhaps

*

today among wintry browns of sedge
dried heather and unnameable pale grasses
and sphagnum moss whose crimson and chartreuse
cushions you can sink your fingers in
to clutch the cold softness of water
and breathe the gentle acrid smell of
peat and damp vegetation

was a sharp shock of colours
scarlet and yellow warning signs
on a cache of black plastic containers labelled
FENCE POST FINISHING KIT
bursting out of a plastic sack that shed
white flakes like old paint   liberated
from the rigours of chemical waste disposal

*

once upon a time a cabinet office meeting
discussed a paper on dispersal
of the soviet nuclear arsenal
I asked why the analysis of each danger
didn't include a risk assessment
of probability and impact
to help us prioritise
and the dark suits looked at me as if
at an alien
afterwards I didn't pursue the principle
being too busy doing my job

once upon a time at a team awayday
we had to step into a four-paned window
taped on the floor   the aim being

to find out our preferences for where
to stand in a team space   I was
the leader and stood at an edge
I felt I could see more clearly from there
did this make me a bad leader

*

once upon a time there was a ghost
in the big house where we were guests
on our first visit to the first island
a chieftain   they said   lay under the hillock nearby
his broadsword hung in the hall
its long sweep of metal dull and pocked
and the edge when I fingered it   blunt
if you touch a sword it should cut you
then an adult explained how
wielded with force it would take your head off

one night everyone went to a ceilidh
leaving my little sister and me
alone with nightlights flickering
shapes onto varnished pitch-pine walls
the grown-ups would be crossing the wheatfield
unlatching the five-barred metal gate with moulded
end-posts and cream paint bled pink by rust
and walking down the dark cloud of the woods

*

sleepless was the wait for the ghost who
arrived on a blast of air
in that still night

and blew out the nightlights
was there   was there   there was
someone there

*

long after they died my sister and I found out that
granny had lost her adored older cousin
in the first world war and our other grandfather
was the only one out of four irish brothers
to survive   this story may not be true

our mother did tell us she and granny
each had a son   born dead
german measles scarlet fever
after she died we found
among old birth and death certificates
an undertaker's bill for a small white coffin

as for grandad I used to talk to him
during his morning bath and would admire
the swirl of flesh on his chest where
shell fragments lurked
missed his artery by a hair
then in the steam and smell of old spice
I'd watch in the mirror
his foamy face half clown half ghost

*

uphill
after lifting a gate of thick wood slats to make

a gap to squeeze through
and walking between rock-face and lochan
I have to avoid one of hell's entrances
a circle that's an unnatural
for here unnatural bright green   not grass
but soupy with duckweed
and in it half submerged
lie a sheep skull and some vertebrae
the skull angled to look like an
anamorphic human one
a daily vanitas

in our purple-and-white uniforms
a loathsome impenetrable shade of purple
sitting on little bentwood chairs
with turquoise metal legs and rubber feet
looking at picture after picture of clocks
we learnt time could be measured and told
and would run on for us
in a straight line

how could we in that classroom have known
life speeds us up
barely noticeable at first   but now
the days running through my hourglass have abraded
the wall of its narrow waist
so they flow faster
widening the gap further

will I become my mother who in old age would say
when asked if she'd done her hip exercises
I haven't had time

*

to eat lunch without having achieved anything
is normal   the visuals are fading
and to access the world requires notice

an egg   that should be a fine thing
now seems ignoble
degraded by association   an omen

pessimism of the intellect
and   or
optimism of the will

rolling hither and thither   hither and thither
through the chances
of being the future's laughing-stock

if you start filling a notebook
from the back
will it tell you what comes next

*

imprisoned not only by a human lifeline
the decay of somatic cells
but inside our bounds and habits of thought
how to train the mind to think in epochs
the ones ending in -cene
like a fast-forward satellite view of
seasons in a temperate zone
colours shivering across the land from snow to
brown to green to wheaten yellow to orange
against blue-grey ocean

not the anthropocene's fiery orange
instead these are the subdued colours
of the ribbed plasticine bars
that I could never keep apart   thumbing them
cack-handedly into one failed animal
shape after another   they'd warm up
giving off a pungent clayey smell
swirl like a river delta
and blend into muddy brown

*

sometimes I don't want   can't bear
to read any more
to think

*

just as time mills things ever smaller with the years
and mixes up the grains
how to train the mind to stay afloat
above the epochs   on the scale of galaxies
aware that the remarkable
green era that nurtured us
won't last forever anyway
would this take me beyond the dark

darkness of childhood terror
dreams of lions   lions because my first
cinema trip was to see
born free   my mother cupped her hand over my eyes
her hand's dry coolness

darkness in the already dark
a woman was washing garments in the river
while a lioness stalked
closer and closer through thick trees
my mother took her hand away too soon I saw
saw the blood floating
a wavy line on the muddy water

we are all prey we are eating each other we have
eaten our young rather than change our lives
how can they keep
the world's zoo easy in their mind
without knowing there's something wrong
let alone the very concept of a zoo

will even zoos save my okapi
her striped hindquarters mimicking slats of light
that fall through leaves
in her upland rainforest

endangered   population decreasing
continuing decline in area extent
and/or quality of habitat   human
settlement   deforestation   degradation
illegal armed groups prevent effective
conservation   engage in and facilitate
elephant poaching   hunting for bushmeat and skins
*   snares   mining   logging   charcoal   agricultural*
encroachment   do they have any
better choices   *one third of the okapi's*
known distribution is likely to be
at risk during the first quarter of
this century   the okapi is the congo's
national animal   rangers in the
okapi wildlife reserve have been murdered

our gold   our diamonds   my columbite-
tantalite known as coltan a dull metallic ore
vital for mobile phones and laptops
setting the conditions for
rangers   forest   okapi

who can trace how far back our thoughts of disaster stretch
from a pinprick of a capillary
through the veins of population explosion
nuclear winter and extinction
all converging in an oily flood of nightmare

*

plunging into the sea disentangles the brain
very cold

your body quails against
the shock
intake of breath

ice's fiery embrace
half-holds you
half-lets go

the horizon splutters
hills into waves
wavelets hill-high

swim out to the buoy
let the mountains
settle on the water's sill

while you balance
half-on   half-in
a liquid plain

green-blue straight down
deep
let it sway you

put its salt taste
to your lips
its damp breath

swim back
spin the sky under sea over
coldness

and plunge out
run along the beach
tall above yourself

numb hands salt damp
tangle clothes and hair

*

lichen calms the heart   it doesn't move
allowing a long look
at its paint chart spun slow-motion from the earth's core
orange   charcoal   ash-grey   yellow
whitewash-spill
and pale unearthly blueish-green

and the mountains
the mountains that lined last year's view

never blue from there all the blue is taken
by a swathe of sea
which leaves them purple and grey sometimes almost black
zig-zagging across the horizon
trace with your eyes the precipice that's just
off vertical an elephant's head
bulbous and swooping
sheer drops can happen at any moment
from what looks entirely normal ground   or you might
lurch into a hidden bog hole
on that slope so smooth from far off with a few
elephant wrinkles but when you walk it

you'll be squelching almost wading through bog and tussocks
no path except deer-paths that never go your way
in spring your ears will be donged
by the golden plover's bell   you'll be
overfluttered by pipit   overflown
by white-tailed eagle or golden   by raven and crow
throwing their own trajectories high above
mountain-trajectories ridge on ridge that you can map
when you get to the top
where the air is sharp and cold as water
if it's a good day you'll see island after island

if you have exceptional luck you might
see a mountain hare whose pelt in spring
still carries patches of the snow
last to melt in a corrie's deep shade

after the descent you may have a long walk out
through dusk unsettled by the small sounds of night
in their season the stags will bellow crag to crag
far above you   back at each other's echo

*

if you walk the high north end cliffs you may
come to an abrupt stop
sheep-cropped grass until the
    drop
to an inlet whose opposite cliff
under its thin crust of earth
exposes the pressure of rocks underfoot
deep deep down to where it's rock-meltingly hot

from space our fires might burn like new volcanic arcs
pustules bubbling up and bursting
even here crofters set light to the heather
for new grazing   but the wind
can blow the flames beyond their control
what if the fires above
join up with the fire from below

I went down the eleven-hour tunnel of the night
and got off the train to find london
smeared in oil and soot   the air
acrid the sky between rooftops a smudge
left by a greasy finger

*

when I struck a long match
to light the gas
the flame flared yellow

but shrank to a blue halo
and sputtered out
so what if   I thought

the whole world's aflame
in a few weeks' time
and the box is empty

will I go hungry
for want of one last match
to light the gas

***   ***   ***

deep winter   some days it is difficult
to go out   and once out I don't want
to turn back   instead to walk
and walk   following a mirage
my body walking the length of its blood vessels
swing of the hips sway of the spine weight of the head
legs a pair of compasses
below balancing arms
and scrambling up rocks the body is all ape
arms made to reach out and hands to
feel for the smallest crack or angle to give purchase
a fingertip-hold so legs   can lever the body up

outlined against low cloud
a crow perched on the shrunken trig-point
    is a raven

during a plunge through heather and frozen bog
where pool surfaces are contour-marked in white
and ice gives way with a rasp
a tall figure appears on a nearby skyline and
my heart   somersaults
    an erratic boulder
balanced there since the ice age
as long as the root of my fear

coffee-grounds stuck under a fingernail
flicked out
a grain of ethiopia in the peat

slosh jump mince stride up-trudge hop swing half-skip
sideways-polka down a slope
all punctuated by the sniff
of a nose runny in cold wind
I should learn to blow it with my other hand
as my mother who once walked miles
never could   she had to stop
to move her stick from right to left

a trip is a stumble to ground level but a tip
would pivot on the body's tipping point
a dive with no water to break your fall
the world swerved
out of orbit

the way it swerves if you board the viking ship
a giant swing in the helsinki funfair
on a hilltop   the skyline distant   the ship
lifts and drops on waves of air
with the creak and groan of wood
until reeling to and fro
through 180 degrees you the crew all
hang   paused
the horizon vertical

as the moon's was when apollo 8
rounded its pale cliff-face to discover a
small blue half-circle shining   inlaid with a white swirl
of cloud   afloat in darkness

they rotated the photo 90 degrees
grounding you the moon your floor
    rotate it back again
to tread on nothing
below you the whole universe

*

islanders evicted to the east were permitted
to return with their dead
because only on the west side
was the soil deep enough for burial
a long walk up their path over the island's backbone
with a mere rucksack

to the beach where   later   blue above the dunes
the sky doesn't seem to darken
but the moon gets brighter

*

open a drawer to the sea's petticoat
layer on layer of white lace ruffles
scalloping beige as they flatten across the sand

when the tide's in flood
walk the waterline and look back
to face unprinted ground

or

in the tale of invisible footsteps
you're crossing an empty beach
on sand marked with bird forklets

at the end you turn by the rocks
and see footprints parallel to yours
moving in your first direction

so you turn round again
no-one there
against the high black rocks

*

uphill after snowfall to bathe
in the brightness and scan the mainland's chain of
white sails stretching north between blue sea and sky
on and on until tarnished by haze

the desire to scrunch through a pure white stretch
must be repressed   in case of bog holes

another day the weather is experimental
exuberantly modelling gulf stream collapse
a frozen band on the sea loch
glutinous icing poured over intertidal rocks
sugary   lickable
the fisher who moors by a disused fish-farm pontoon
whose collie stands figurehead front paws on the gunwhale
had to break ice
to go out and lift the pots

in a bill from the shop
the scrubber that curves to a point at one end

is itemised as   boat-shaped brush
you hold it by the keel

*

these clear nights I go outside to greet
orion due south opposite the door
mid-stride in a wheeling smirr of stars

life spirals inward each week's circuit
a little smaller than the last
evenings only distinguished from night by the clock
lights on for hours warming the wooden walls and roof-slope
windows a dark line of oblongs
giving nothing back
except the echo of wind and rain
and the white square of an open book
clearer than its ghostly reader
or reflections of vera   small axe   dealbhan fraoich
mingulay in black and white with the gaelic
voices of its people who had to leave their island
so storm-tossed it was hard to get ashore and
says one voice on the crackling tape
we had no fuel left
we had dug all the peat

here we are diesel-powered since the big cable
got damaged   the navy   the russians   who knows
and the wind farms had to be stilled

*

birds are flying like scraps   scraps like birds
the island roars with a gale
besieged on all sides by foam

a raft of eider ducks rides it out
wintering off the west beaches
kaleidoscope of brown-white-dark
against deep blue

how is it possible to get up
from a chair   stand full height
walk the still air from table to sink
when the wind if it hissed and thumped
any harder would blow the house inside out
fridge   sofa   large white plates   books
teabags   polyethylene-wrapped vegetables
nothing local except the eggs
all flying   torn away
through horizontal hail that mills outdoors to a blur

if the island could upend and dive
with a flip of its tail
how deep down would the storm go with it

on a bare cliff-top where the wind howls
and both legs walk away from the body
out of context   springs a ewe
who stares   glares at me   staring at her
amber eyes in a black face rorschach-blotted white
chewing sideways   standing foursquare
her horns curved like handles to an ancient pitcher
balancing her with the dignity of a headdress

when I walk along the sea loch to the big bins
after one gale and before another
next door's sheep mob me   gently

smelling of lanolin
when I open the plastic sack and show them
old newspapers and yogurt pots
they peer inside   sceptical   the sack says
their supplementary pellets contain soya
so are these wind- and rain-blown sheep
munching away at tropical rainforest

the man in the silver SUV wasn't
hooting to let the end of the road know he's here
but to notify his flock
they come bouncing over the lumpy ground
off-white and smoky brown
draughts from an upturned board
to eat the feed he tips from a blue bucket

*

on rough ground above the loch
in a rare clump of bog myrtle
bare-branched

a subsong a song thrush
rehearsing
under its breath digging out of winter

*

in march in the long afterwinter
in upland pools frogspawn floats
a cloudy slick on the peaty dark of bog holes
bulging like a plastic bag out of the water

always in deep pools that will not dry out
or flood away in downpours   the tadpoles
mere dots in their jelly will make snipe-food later
some are elongating   growing tails
dagger blade to the head's hilt
first comma today   it wriggled

this morning when the door opened the air smelt of earth
a warm smell in the nostrils despite the late march cold
birdsong   catkins   twin lambs
seen by the bus driver very small and early
a neighbour's daffodil buds are greenish-yellow
last year the sheep got in and ate the lot

snow of the lambs they say in gaelic
sneachd nan uan
snow brightens the taller grasses that stick out
brown   green   straw-pale   dark red
drooping heads with long blond tassels
a tuft of dried stems each topped by a seed-bobble
that sways with its own weight

snowflakes when small jink in the wind like gnats
and veil the hills in smoke
big flakes fall straight in flocks of thousands each one
an   O   the last surprise
taken in silence
against the blanked-out view

*

among stunted trees behind the next house
one croft-width away
a blackbird's begun to sing

notes flowing like wine
after a winter of water
echoing over the loch

*

the wheatear smartly patterned
hopping stone to stone
finds his full voice   his reedy trill
a female has arrived
tinged with a rose wash that both dulls and warms her
they hop together in the sun and he sings in bursts
until thud   thud
he attacks a rival in the window glass

after next day's blizzard
she's disappeared
flown from central africa has she
succumbed to the renewed cold too windy for gnats
or merely given up on him
he's gone quiet again
hopping from one stone rib to another
of the ruins inside which this house nestles
walls at chest height
topped by moss and stonecrop and grasses
that wave against the sky
with sea loch filling the old door and window spaces

big oblong stones of stripey gneiss   a bookcase
of rock   books stacked vertically and in piles
the wheatear's crevice explorations turn the wall
inside out   his desire lines form a cast
for a rachel whiteread monument

but oh his vanished mate
his possibly window-addled brain
another snow squall
looming dark across the sea

*

the air's turned hazy
sometimes almost warm   easier to stop
at bog-pools   a pond-skater's feet
make six sunlit dents on the surface
and its shadow on the pool's peaty floor
forms a paw-print edged with gold
is this how the skater looks to the tadpoles
grown out of their squirming nursery
into eyed spheres with a tarnished froggy gleam
trying out their tails in squiggly forays
soon they will break the lid of the surface
haul themselves out of the slime

very very slowly across the floor of one pool
moves an enormous creature a medieval
siege engine   a warhorse fully armoured
back home the online guide to pond life has
nothing half the size or one-tenth
as terrifying

*

headlights catch
and sear silver
an otter's undulation

seesaw lolloping
the shock
of animal motion

out of pitch dark
spotlit
a run of old negatives

*

on windy days the sky is extravagant
such depth to the layers of cloud
today they formed rainforest hills
above a steep valley wreathed in steam

among cliff-top trees   dark cloud-puffs
the okapi swivels her large soft black-fringed
butterfly-wing ears   unloops her tentacular
blue tongue and extends it
upwards to grasp a tongueful of leaves
okapi creature of forest and made of leaves
her eyes deep brown pools   impenetrable
her conker-bright hide   cream stockings   neat hooves
with scent glands to mark her route   her secret
language of infrasonic calls
shy and elusive as [she] is serene and gentle
the one close relative of the giraffe
who was my mother's favourite
long and gangly   like us

after the rain a walk by the loch
in the gap between two online meetings
past the strung-out houses

and white metal squares on poles at passing-places
knowing that the longer I unreel
the thread of the road
the more it will need reeling back in
   too far
despite the socks in my wellies
rucking under the soles of my feet
up to the hillock before the next township
overlooking the sea

if you walk along a road you can't stop
anywhere and turn back
you need a topographical reason

on a rock islet cormorants hold
their wings out wide to dry
further out shafts of white sun
patch the grey water
and make a glittery snowglobe
of gulls wheeling through a squall of hail

the next meeting is about london's filthy air
the fight to breathe in my own borough
where I'll have to return soon

easy to have a bad conscience the question is
what to do with it   how absurd it felt
to have to put our bodies on the airport road
hundreds of cassandras getting arrested
there must be a better way   but now
the sea loch's long gash and
puddles in the bog and on the road
are throwing enough of the sky back
for it not to feel dark yet

on the outward part of a final walk
you are still going somewhere

*

will it be like waking from a dream
or will life never not feel like a dream ever again
have I swayed too far   to return

*

early today a stillness hung in the air
spring and the next-door sheepdog's barking
echoed hill to hill as the barks
of the wild and toothy farm dogs
echo off the slope of a stone mountain
that crowns another island far away
in a near-landlocked sea
the inside out of here
a sea whose hard-edged islands at first repelled me
used to the cloudy softness of the north

there spring starts in winter
wild daffodils snake along the river
through the village named river
asphodel break a pale mist out of the dry hillside
and anemones' pure pigments
splash the ground   mauve   deep purple
white   shell and fuchsia pink   black-centred scarlet
pale and royal blue and rarest midnight

early morning goat-bells
the farmer whistling half bach half folk
a cupboard door shudders open

beach towels tumble out with a smell of plaster
unfurling faded patterns

by now high on that mountain
clumps of heartsease will be glowing
inside crown-of-thorns
and remnants of the oak wood shaking out
yellow-green leaves to hide its gnarled contortions
goats gnaw any seedlings while the mountain's
other side is being eaten away
by quarrying for patio stones
and far below lorry-loads of rubbish are dumped
in the marshy lagoon
where migratory birds stop over

*

but here the wheatear has fallen
down the chimney
after attacking the shiny chimney-pot
clanging echoed down the stovepipe   it went very quiet
through the cold ashy glass of the stove door
an upright bird-shape perched
still as a stuffed bird under a bell-jar

*

sea-mist
one field away on all sides
dirty sheep

*

a box of 80
teabags shouldn't go this fast
or is it the days

*

life is easing as the sun's arc widens
such pleasure to walk again in company
talking about how much incomers are
paying to buy houses   why the council
is all-male   ferry trouble   livestock prices
whose cuckoos have returned this week
here one arrived mid-april far side of the loch
to send its echo across   now there's a second
to echo back

lambs are out   bleating
escaping under fences unable to get back
once you've cornered a lamb
grabbed a fistful of fleece
holding on tight because it will try to run
and picked it up
it will go limp and fit roundly under your arm

the first dot of violet on the hill was a shock
mistaken for plastic   now there's a scattering
milkwort is flowering deep blue or pale
and curly pink lousewort   a few bumble bees
water-pale orchids with crimson code-marks

the purple flaglet of butterwort rising
from a lime-green starfish of insect-eating leaves
    but   it seems   few insects
yellow tormentil   shiny yellow celandine
soon outshone by kingcups bursting out of ditches

how powerfully colours imprint themselves
on eyes that saw none for half a year

now the lochans are sprouting with
whiteish-pink flowering bogbean
and large dark waterlily leaves mirroring the sun
    tew-tew-tew   mind where you walk
    two greenshank fly up
on the sea loch greylags parade fuzzy goslings
single file with an adult at each end

otter spraint spattered on a grassy pad
hidden among rocks by the shore

snipe thrum over evening air not quite dark
doppler effect as they pass

on the west side the machair blooms
its early colours   yellow and white
and along the sand waders mark the water's edge
attenuated
one curlew

*

an egg
beautiful egg   large
a broken feast

black ink spots and blotches
across a shell
the colour of wet sand

split and emptied
on steep grass
among squill and primrose

where below the cliff
two oystercatchers
nest among dark rocks

scattered with pale barnacles
and lichen   black pebbles
dotting the sand

between one and four
eggs are laid
typically three

***   ***   ***

am I really here
in gaelic they say in an island not on it
link in the chain of shapes once searched for
in the blue-gold haze
though we could never see so far north
to this stark land
mostly treeless
softened now by the flowers

you can imagine how it might be here without sheep
from the islets in lochs that are thick
with gorse and rowan and birch

it's hard living without trees   their shape in winter
the dimension they add to landscape
their multiplication of its surface area
most of all to walk among beings larger than human
to be calmed as they slow down time

hard not to stroke the buds and crumpled leaves
emerging in a small plantation along the road
longing for the stunted trees to rustle
can their mycorrhizal network reach the lone rowan
halfway up a stone precipice near the shore
branches twisted and gesturing
as if to ask the sky   what

*

early june and the blackbird
has stopped singing
from the ruined crofthouse where feral cats roam

the blackbird
who filled the long pale evenings with his music

the blackbird

*

sea-lurched   spray-soaked
thinking only of water
but finding fire

a fractured circle
of jagged rock
a graph of extremes

or ocean waves above the ocean
steep slopes felted in green
one hillside traced

with drystone runes
and inked with the legendary
single line of houses

smart-drone bonxies attack
on the ridge where a radar station
mimics the domed cleits

a wren lands on a stone
sings   differently
and with guano and sea pinks

on an outcrop of this outpost
puffins   sweet rainbows
are nesting

   as we leave
cold waves boil
around the impossible stacs

*

parts of the loch shore are a repository
for a sea-spectrum of ropes
dark blue turquoise beige and orange
coils and nets that fray into wormy strands

unghostly gear
and for plastic bottles and canisters
their brighter bottle-tops
and near the road sweet-wrappers and cans and
a few whisky and beer bottles
a neighbour says her children used to find
small bottles made of deep blue glass

chunks of polystyrene buoy-filler
and their nurdles like fish roe shining in the bog
gloves off to fingernail-pick these out
they appear in the excrement of shore-birds

from half a mile of indented coastline
two dozen extra large binbags
plus three stashes of stuff too big to collect
septic tank drums   huge plastic jerrycans from fish farms
and fat hawsers to moor you
against the wildest storm

an inventory long as the loch
the only prize a small picnic mug in sludgy green
with a ridged handle and
plastics by NBC limited   on the base
the word   plastics   in diminishing letters
framed by an oblong
to herald the future's excitement
the whole mug is lopsided maybe from the bog
it still has that old-fashioned smell
that would get into your tea

on the hill swathes of bog-cotton bright as snow

*

last night I kept from sleep
and willed myself
to dream of him

for the last conversation
we never had
while knowing that dreams

bring back the dead
randomly   as the sea
lands flotsam

   in the small hours
his time
I dreamt a surface

strewn with twisted shapes
as if the dozen herring
cross-hatched in silver

on his wooden tray
propped up on a bookcase
had leapt out

   he was there
though his gravelly drawl
hesitant   sardonic   held close

in my mind's ear
was wordless
and his long frame was tilted

between slanting walls
of a watery house   was it his
tilted at the angle

of luskentyre graveyard
behind the dunes
   where a gale

whipped sand in our faces
off the long neat pile
as the minister called out

against its roar and the unseen
breaking waves
the full names of six men

who stepped forward one by one
took hold of three ropes
and let his coffin down

*

is it possible to be in the real island and the dream island
at the same time
   to inhabit the real as if in that haze
   or inhabit the haze as if real

*

all I knew of my okapi
was her miniature plastic likeness
faded over time from dark brown
to plum colour   some rubbed off
widening her white stripes into patches
I didn't even pronounce her right
until remembering her   first time since childhood
speakers of mvuba in north-eastern congo

revere her   named her   in english it's
okapi with the a as in hardly
not to rhyme with the baby she has in a video
so scarce   zoo-born in safety yet nothing
of home but her name   to which the name of a
british   discoverer   has been appended

my okapi was solitary
unlike the showier animals
at least that's how I remember her
I used to put her to graze under the shade
of the oak from the farm set whose plugged-in branches
you could strip for a winter scene

if at the end
I still have mind and memory
might it be possible to go back to
the lawn and lie there young and clean
     under a blue sky
     almost reachable
eye level with bees and ants the flowers tickling my nose
dandelion   black medic   speedwell   tormentil
red and sweet-smelling white clover
chickweed or was it stitchwort or both
and the scarlet pimpernel
that had to be looked for

the houses in my grandparents' road were built
in the 1930s on the then outskirts
on meadowland
and years later it came to me
those flowers that could miniaturise must have done so
over decades to survive the mower's blade
might it be possible to hold on
to that thought
and not ask myself if the lawn's still like that
are the flowers still there

NOTES

p.8 'that island': Eigg in the Inner Hebrides.

p.10 'captain... postmistress', p.16 'neighbours', and
throughout: I have not named anyone in the poem,
out of respect and reticence, island communities being
relatively small.

p.11 'sun and shadow': West Harris in the Western Isles
or Outer Hebrides.

pp.16-17 Gaelic phrases:
Good morning, how are you?
It's windy today.
Indeed it is.

p.21 'the red of a diver's long throat... one great
northern's': red-throated diver and great northern diver.

p.22 'late autumn on the east side': the Bays of Harris,
facing the Minch and the cliffs of Skye.

p.23 'islanders/ evicted': a brief history and much other
material is at https://hebridespeople.com/

p.34 'endangered... encroachment': language from the
International Union for Conservation of Nature's report
at https://www.iucnredlist.org/species/15188/51140517.
The okapi was last assessed in 2015.

p.34 'one third... century': from the same IUCN page,
quoting a 2013 paper by J A Hart.

p.34 'rangers... murdered': in 2023, two Congolese rangers
were murdered in the Okapi Wildlife Reserve in the

north-east of the Democratic Republic of the Congo.
In 2017, four rangers and a porter were murdered. In
2012, seven people, including villagers and rangers,
were murdered at the Okapi Conservation Project
headquarters, along with all the okapi there. Local
rebel groups carrying out illegal mining and poaching
are held responsible. This article gives some idea of the
complexity of the situation: https://news.mongabay.
com/2023/10/its-a-real-mess-mining-and-deforestation-
threaten-unparalleled-drc-wildlife-haven/

p.44 'dealbhan fraoich': Heather's Portraits, a TV
programme that's good for Gaelic learners (BBC Alba
has English subtitles).

p.50 'shy... gentle': from https://www.okapiconservation.
org/the-okapi – a good source of okapi information.

p.51 'another island far away': southern Evia, Greece.

p.57 'sea-lurched': visiting St Kilda, whose main bay is a
flooded volcanic caldera.

ACKNOWLEDGEMENTS

Thanks to my poetry gang – Joanna Clark, Jan Kofi-Tsekpo, Jeri Onitskansky, Selina Rodrigues and Ali Thurm – for their comments on *Okapi*, their encouragement and for being there, always.

Thanks to Colin Hughes, Mimi Khalvati and Nell Nelson for their comments on earlier versions of the manuscript, and to the Torriano Poetry Workshop for their close reading of various passages.

Thanks to Victoria Rance for help with the cover.

Thanks to editor & publisher Rob A Mackenzie, for believing in *Okapi*.

Thanks to Pete Godfrey for making *Okapi* and much else possible by asking me to house-sit, and to Paul Munro & Annalie Sinfield for renting me their lovely house at Leac a Lì over the second winter.

Thanks to all in Harris and Lewis who welcomed me with such kindness. Special thanks to Mary & Donald MacDonald in Horgabost, and to members of the Hebridean Walking Club.

In memory of Julian Ward, neighbour in Leac a Lì. He was the last of the group of three elders who walked together, in Harris years ago and elsewhere, so also in memory of the other two, Lesley Gowans and Meryl Moore.

Any profits the author makes from *Okapi* (£5 per book at cover price) will be divided between two charities:

Clean Coast Outer Hebrides: "An environmental charity whose mission is to protect the coastline of the Outer Hebrides. Our vision is to end coastal pollution around our islands. We engage tourists and the local community, lead beach cleans, deliver educational outreach sessions to schools and community groups, and host environmental discussions." cleancoastoh.com.

Rainforest Foundation UK: "Our mission is to support indigenous peoples and other communities of the world's rainforest in their efforts to protect their environment and fulfil their rights to land, life and livelihood." rainforestfoundationuk.org/

Fiona Moore lives in Greenwich, London. Her first collection, *The Distal Point* (HappenStance Press, 2018), was a Poetry Book Society recommendation and shortlisted for the T S Eliot prize and the Seamus Heaney first collection prize. Before this she published two pamphlets, also with HappenStance: *The Only Reason for Time*, a Guardian poetry book of the year in 2013, and *Night Letter*, shortlisted for the 2015 Michael Marks Award.

She is a member of *Magma*'s editorial board, editing issues themed for climate change (2018) and islands (2023). Before that she was assistant editor at *The Rialto*. She is part of the group reviving Poetry in Aldeburgh for 2024. She campaigns on climate and environmental issues.

Okapi, her second book, comes out of nearly two years living in the Outer Hebrides.